WARREN KIMBLE
American Folk Artist

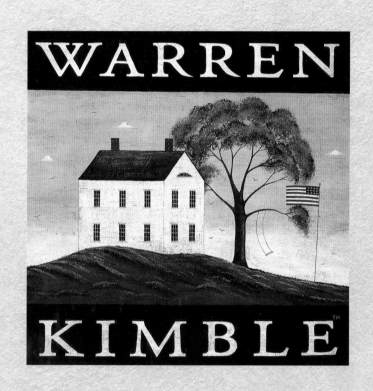

His Life, His Art & Collections
With Inspirations and Patterns for
Creative American Folk Crafts

Copyright© 2000 by Landauer Corporation

Art Copyright© 2000 by Warren Kimble®
This book was designed, produced, and published by Landauer Books
A division of Landauer Corporation
12251 Maffitt Road, Cumming, Iowa 50061

President: Jeramy Lanigan Landauer
Vice President: Becky Johnston
Managing Editor: Marlene Hemberger Heuertz
Art Director: Laurel Albright
Creative Director: Margaret Sindelar
Photographers: Craig Anderson and Amy Cooper
Illustrator: Stewart Cott

This book is printed on acid-free paper.

Printed in China

Library of Congress Cataloging-in-Publication Data

Kimble, Warren.
   Warren Kimble American folk artist: his life, his art & collections with inspirations for creative American folk crafts/Warren Kimble.
      p.cm. – (Signature artist series from Landauer)
   ISBN 1-890621-09-9 (hc.)
      1. Kimble, Warren. 2. Kimble, Warren–Homes and haunts. 3. Interior decoration–United States–History–20th century. 4. Decoration and ornament, Rustic–United States. 5. Decorative arts–United States–History–20th century. I. Title: Warren Kimble, American Folk Artist. II. Title. III. Series.

ND237.K52 A4 1999
745'.0973–dc21
                                                              99-042501

DEDICATION

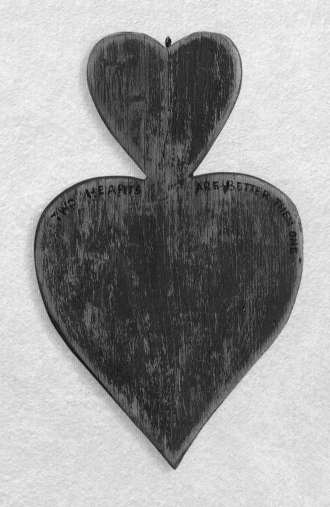

Lorraine...

Two Hearts are Better Than One.

Forever, Warren

"Once neglected and almost beyond repair,
this nineteenth-century barn now serves as
my studio and source for inspiration."

FOREWORD

One of the greatest joys of my life has been to share my world with visitors who come to see my studio and gallery in Brandon, Vermont.

I really enjoy showing visitors an environment where antiques and collectibles from the past are part of everyday modern life. It's also a pleasure to tell my guests about the history and origin of the artwork and crafts which they encounter.

My hope is that this book offers you the opportunity to get to know these surroundings better and to learn their history.

I feel very fortunate to be able to live and work surrounded by the rolling hillsides of Vermont. Here, the four seasons as well as the rich animal and plant life offer each of us the chance to experience something larger and more beautiful than ourselves. I hope the opportunity arises when you can visit us. When you do, I will be delighted to welcome you to this special place.

CONTENTS

*"It's crazy but it's wonderful . . .
I am living my dream!"*

INTRODUCTION

The world of Warren Kimble is delightfully simple and welcoming. In a restored nineteenth-century barn that serves as his studio, Warren offers visitors the chance to see arts, antiques, and rare items that reflect a lifetime of painting and collecting. Now regarded as America's best known living folk artist, Warren Kimble continues to work as he has done for the past forty years. By painting everyday and maintaining an active role in his community, Warren Kimble has demonstrated what one critic has said are priorities in the right order: "Good folks and good folk art."

Warren Kimble's early love for painting is evident in this oil painting of poppies and delphiniums painted when he was 13 years old.

Warren Kimble was often the "life of the party." For this birthday celebration, he leads the parade of mostly happy revelers.

Warren spent his summers in a cottage by the sea.

Fun times included folding newspapers to make paper hats with his childhood friend, Nancy Littlewood Hallock.

Seascapes and landscapes are major themes in Warren Kimble's art. Warren attributes much of this to summers spent at the family's cottage on the New Jersey seashore and at his grandparents' farm in Monroe, New Jersey. Raised in Belleville, New Jersey, this city boy developed a life-long love for the sea and the countryside as a result of these early influences.

Warren vividly recalls those summers spent without the distractions of television and video games as the golden opportunity to develop his independence and focus his energy on creative activities such as drawing, painting, and sand-sculpting.

"Though I couldn't keep the big old rocking chair that belonged to my Aunt Nellie for so many years, I was able to replicate it in charcoal for future generations to enjoy."

"I can still recall the rustling breeze and reflections of the trees in the rippling waters of the pond on the Kimble Family Farm."

Proud to be featured as the head cheerleader for Syracuse University in this photo from the 1955 yearbook, Warren joined other alumni at a reunion weekend football game in 1998. Warren jokingly notes that he is wearing less hair, but now at least what remains matches his sweater!

Warren Kimble's barn studio is home to many valuable collectibles, but the value he places on his Syracuse University keepsakes is far greater than anything money can buy. As a 1957 graduate of Syracuse University, Warren Kimble feels strongly that the education he received there contributed significantly to the success he enjoys today.

The first member of his family to attend college, Warren was encouraged to apply to Syracuse University by a friend at the end of his senior year in high school. In addition to majoring in fine arts, Warren Kimble immersed himself in a wide range of social activities at Syracuse. He was President of both his Junior and Senior class, and personally received his degree from then-Senator John F. Kennedy, who delivered the Commencement address.

In addition to being a member of the Lambda Chi fraternity, Warren Kimble was also the Head Cheerleader at Syracuse from his sophomore through his Senior year. Among his most memorable experiences was cheering at the 1957 Cotton Bowl football game.

"To this day, I continue to be a loyal Syracuse fan, a dedicated alumnus, and goodwill ambassador for the University."

Throughout his 21-year teaching career, which included kindergarten to college, Warren Kimble never lost his love for painting. He continued to sketch, draw, and paint purely for his own satisfaction.

Relocating from Pompton Plains, New Jersey to the small town of Brandon, Vermont in 1970, Warren renewed his love for the country and began painting rural landscapes and pastoral scenes which included the dairy cows which dot the hillsides of Vermont.

Warren Kimble's love for country in his paintings begins with the very surface on which he paints. First-time visitors to Warren Kimble's studio are often surprised to learn about the "canvas" on which he paints. Rather than painting on barn board, which is too rough for the definition his images require, Warren prefers to paint on old tabletops, cupboard doors, and bread boards.

These old boards, which were once a useful part of someone's home, provide just the right amount of distressed texture for his art.

While working as a teacher and collector and dealer, Warren Kimble continued to paint, often at night.

Warren Kimble transforms a diverse collection of discarded doors, tabletops, cutting boards, and picture frames into a treasury of primitive folk art.

With the old boards serving as his canvas, and after thirty years of experience painting in different techniques, a new style began to evolve for Warren Kimble that resulted in a portfolio of folk art paintings.

Now considered to be some of his most famous works, these paintings were initially produced for his own enjoyment and relaxation.

The paintings would have remained part of his private collection had they not been exhibited at Gallery on the Green in Woodstock, Vermont. The owners (two young entrepreneurs), Laurie and John Chester, saw the exhibition and included "Kissing Cows" in their affordably-priced Wild Apple Graphics collection of prints.

"When we bought this old relic, it was in total disrepair. But the years of hard work that Lorraine and I put into restoration have resulted in a house worthy of calling "home.""

In addition to working as a teacher, Warren Kimble also devoted a considerable amount of time to the restoration and sale of nineteenth-century homes in Brandon, Vermont. These projects provided Warren and his wife, Lorraine Kimble, with the opportunity to indulge in their passion for decorating and remodeling. The town of Brandon (population 4,000) also has some of the best architecture in the state of Vermont, due largely to its attraction as a summer resort in the nineteenth century for persons of means.

The Kimbles have renovated more than a dozen houses in Brandon, including their present home (shown above). At the start of this project, even the ever- optimistic Warren Kimble was apprehensive about the condition of the house and wondered if all the effort would be worth the investment. However, upon tearing off the ugly shingles and the sagging front porch, they discovered the original clapboards as well as details such as dentil molding above the door. From then on, it was a labor of love to bring back the beauty of this 1810 Colonial, which has been home to Warren and Lorraine for the past 13 years. The small garden shed and the barn which serves as Warren Kimble's studio (opposite) are situated nearby.

ART

America's best-known living folk artist, Warren Kimble paints in a variety of styles ranging from serious studies of fruits and flowers in still life to whimsical sketches of Santas and snowmen.

LANDSCAPES

Four best-known themes of this versatile folk artist— animals, fruits and flowers, landscapes, and patriotism— easily mix and match for the perfect blend of lifestyle decorating.

RED, WHITE & BLUE

ANIMALS

©WARREN KIMBLE

Friendly animals play a major role in Warren Kimble's primitive folk art. His original painting of the "Cock & Bull Inn" featured here is modeled after highly-prized eighteenth-century tavern signs. Since few people in the Colonies could read, it was necessary for landmark inns or taverns to display outdoor signs with easily recognized symbols such as animals, ships, or patriots. This artistic ploy is a tongue-in-cheek example of Warren Kimble's subtle wit and unique sense of whimsy. Another example is the "Games" box topped by a checkerboard painted by Mick Loscalzo.

Adopting the same freedom of style and scale as the early
American folk artists whom he emulates, Warren Kimble's original
painting of a cat is out of proportion but still pleasing to the eye.

With limited resources, Colonial-day artists were often required to grind their
own pigments and mix their own colors of paint using whatever materials they
had on hand. If a particular region boasted unusual variations of clay,
paintings and painted objects from local artisans might be distinguished by the
unique rusty reds and browns of nature's own palette. The shades of paint in
the stack of nesting Shaker boxes from Warren Kimble's collection represent
predominant colors of the day and complement his painting of a feline at play.

Like his Colonial counterparts,Warren Kimble takes license with the
laws of nature and shows an over-sized sow front and center with her
miniature piglets both properly positioned in a surreal setting.
This peaceful and balanced view of the world was of particular importance
to many of the early American folk artists. Surrounded by hardship, poverty,
unforeseen disasters, death and disease, those who
survived chose to make the best of it and then paint the best of it as well.

Warren's paintings of pigs have long been popular with collectors; so too are the
"hog scraper candlesticks" displayed with his original painting. As he explains the
double-duty of these primitive tools, "In the tanning process, the candle
flame was used to singe the hair on the hide. The loosened hog hair could
then be more easily removed using the base of the candlestick as a scraper."

25

One of the most well known animals in Vermont, the Holstein cow is also a frequent subject for Warren Kimble's paintings.

One of his first paintings of Holsteins, "Kissing Cows," portrayed these popular animals in a new, almost whimsical dimension that caught the eye of collectors and popular fans alike.

Immediately published as an open edition print by Wild Apple Graphics, this image began the Warren Kimble success story and continues to represent the classic Warren Kimble "look."

• •

Encouraged by the unexpected success of his "Kissing Cows," Warren continued to paint folk images, branching out into landscapes filled with familiar farm animals, like the horses featured in this original painting. Warren chose to paint in the style reminiscent of nineteenth-century folk art which flourished in Colonial America. Local painters were mostly untrained and based their compositions on personal observations of the landscape. Their desire for balance and harmony is reflected in the frequent use of mirror images and a charming disregard for scale. Thus, the massive stylized horses in the foreground stand in stark contrast to the rural scene of house and trees painted in such smaller scale.

On the farm, hens were highly prized for the eggs—a staple item in the family food supply as well as a source of income for trading or bartering in town for goods and services.

When he first began painting chickens, Warren KImble had no idea how popular they would prove to be with his collectors. Starting with a basic hen which inspired the painting on the tray shown here, Warren expanded his flock to include roosters of all colors, shapes, and sizes. The results have truly become something to crow about! Warren Kimble's hens and roosters regularly appear on numerous licensed products including fabrics, rugs, and fashions.

· ·

For the most part, the rabbit has not been considered a friend for most Vermont farmers since these nocturnal visitors nibble away at profits from the fresh produce being raised for market.

As with his other animals, however, Warren Kimble's painted folk art bunnies have whimsy and have hopped into the hearts and homes of millions of collectors. His original paintings of rabbits have inspired everything from rugs to the carved lamp base by TomLin Designs displayed here on a Warren Kimble original painted tabletop.

FRUITS & FLORALS

WARREN KIMBLE

With his home and studio surrounded by birch trees, flowering shrubs, and perennials, it's easy to see why fruits and flowers are a dominant theme in Warren Kimble's art. Framed by the bay window in the garden room of Warren and Lorraine Kimble's home, the view of birch trees and beds of iris in bloom, appears to be almost picture-perfect.

In the Colonial era, most still life paintings were the domain of young women schooled in the refined arts of needlework, drawing, and painting. After much practice, the resulting "fancy work" was shared with friends and family as decoration for the often drab, colorless walls of early American homes.

For the young women learning to paint, these fruit and floral images were so much in demand that books were written with detailed instructions on how to arrange the elements into a "theorem" as the finished designs came to be called. Even not-so-talented artists were assured a certain measure of success with a steady supply of pre-cut stencils readily available through advertisements in the nineteenth-century ladies' magazines.

In his four original still life paintings of fruits (shown above),
Warren Kimble introduces the handwoven basket as an interesting art element.
Baskets of all shapes and sizes were an indispensible item for early
American households, used for a variety of tasks from shopping to storage.

Basket-making was a time-honored handcraft and a finished basket as
beautiful as it was utilitarian. Warren's fanciful painted
recreations are shown with a round-bottomed basket featuring a unique
and useful swing handle. It is one of several rare baskets
from his collection and likely made in the Taconic region of New York.

. . . .

The themes found in Warren Kimble's art extend beyond farm animals to
include garden scenes, flowers, fruits, and vegetables. "Nature's Bounty"
(shown above) is one such example of the harmony in nature which
Warren illustrates through his paintings of still life. His wife and
business partner, Lorraine Kimble, encouraged her husband to
consider these subjects after the initial success of his paintings of animals.

As a result of Lorraine Kimble's master gardening plan, the splashy

springtime tulips and the showy iris that come up every year are perfect

models for Warren Kimble's detailed botanicals. When Lorraine planted a stand

of slender birches in the side yard and surrounded it with a circular border of

iris, little did she know that it would later provide just the right inspiration for

Warren's "Birchwood" collection of dinnerware which features plates and bowls

bordered by colorful iris clustered against a background of birch bark.

In addition to the dinnerware from Sakura, Warren Kimble's

original paintings of vivid purple iris images

(shown above) are included in a line of art prints published by

Wild Apple Graphics and have blossomed into numerous other products.

LANDSCAPES

Scenes of daily life, landscapes, and

seascapes were popular

subjects of the early American folk

artists who recorded

history through their paintings.

Warren Kimble's paintings

abound with images

of America's rich rural heritage.

For him, landscapes and

seascapes, combined in

the original painting "Coastal Breeze"

featured here, hold particular

interest and have become

several of his favorite themes.

Warren Kimble's landscapes invariably feature stylized trees and rolling hills reminiscent of the rural Vermont countryside where he lives and works. His hometown of Brandon is situated in a broad valley running north and south through central Vermont, lying among beautiful lakes and streams and encircled by mountains.

To many of these landscapes, Warren Kimble adds primitive buildings— a house, barn, church or school— in a variety of shapes and sizes but always in his signature style, like the original painting of "Brandon Barn" (above).

For the distressed look of primitive folk art, he paints landscapes on old cupboard doors and discarded wooden bread boards which provide just the right background texture. When the painting is completed, Warren Kimble often adds a handpainted frame of his own design for another layer of dimension.

Barns surviving from the eighteenth century are extremely rare—the few that remain were well built by the very wealthy. Most people owned only an ox or a horse and a couple of cows with little need for a large barn. Over the years, many of the landmark barns in rural America have outlived their usefulness, fallen into disrepair, and eventually disappeared from the landscape. But Warren Kimble has brought them back—better and often bigger than life.

Since the size, style, and even color of the barns which still remain today
varies from region to region, Warren Kimble's barn paintings are a veritable visual primer.
Although they were often used as social centers for husking bees and dances,
barns were originally built to be hard-working buildings with few frills.
Eleven major ethnic groups introduced various styles brought over from the "old country."
The Germans favored log buildings while the English insisted on timber frame.
Almost all barns are rectangular and built with a round, gambrel or a gable
roof covering a second-story loft for storing hay which requires ventilation to avoid
spontaneous combustion. For ventilation, many of the German barns featured impressive
square cupolas with Victorian-style louvers on each of the four sides capped with ornate
roofs and lightening rods. From the original painting of a simple barn with·silo (shown
above), the barns Warren created for licensed products have
become more elaborate, incorporating a variety of interesting details. Here,
barns trim the sideboard as well as the "Barns" dinnerware collection for Sakura.

41

RED, WHITE & BLUE

The signing of the Declaration of Independence in 1776 ushered in an era of America independence in art forms which inspired paintings "of the people, for the people, and by the people." With patriotism at its peak, the flag, Uncle Sam, and anything red, white, and blue (and later Lincoln and his stovepipe hat) became popular folk art subjects. ("Abe" carved by contemporary folk artist Christopher Lamontagne is an impressive replica.) In keeping with the spirit of America, Warren Kimble counts patriotism as one of his major folk art themes.

• •

Warren Kimble takes pride in his town and takes an active role in
community leadership and development, including leading the annual
Fourth of July parade in Brandon, Vermont. This photo was taken in 1996
by family friend and owner of the historic Brandon Inn, Louis Pattis.

Not just content to fly the flag, Warren Kimble paints folk art interpretations
of stars and stripes in all shapes and sizes to display proudly on the walls
of his studio. The original painting "Three Cheers for the Red, White, and Blue"
(opposite above) is inspired by the Colonial flag and trimmed
with stars for a spirited summer salute to America.

For the thirteen colonies, a flag known as the Continental Colors was flown in January of 1776 with a Union Jack in the upper left corner (the canton) accompanied by thirteen red and white stripes attributed to a radical patriotic group known as the Sons of Liberty.

On June 14, 1777, which later officially became Flag Day, the Union Jack was replaced by a canton of thirteen stars on a blue field. This unusual combination of Stars and Stripes represented a new constellation—The United States of America. When Vermont and Kentucky joined the Union, two new stars and stripes were added. Proving to be too bulky, later the stripes were reduced to 13 with only an additional star added for each new state.

Warren Kimble's "America" flag (shown below) with wheat in the foreground is a highly-stylized interpretation of the present-day American flag. But he still shows respect by painting it according to proper flag etiquette—with the canton of stars seen on the upper left.

For Warren, the simple stars and stripes symbolizing independence represent the spirit of much of what he feels is good about America. A similar freedom from traditional art forms makes it possible for Warren Kimble to share his unique blend of the old and the new with avid folk art collectors not only in America, but around the world.

ANTIQUES
COLLECTIBLES

Each of Warren Kimble's
distinctive folk art painting themes—
animals, fruits and florals,
landscapes, and patriotism—
has been greatly influenced by
treasured antiques and collectibles
that fill his home and heart.

Looking back, Warren Kimble
feels that some of these influences
can be directly traced to favorite
toys and the surroundings of
his early childhood. Especially
memorable are the summertime
visits to the cottage by the
sea and the Kimble Family Farm.

The antiques and collectibles that fill Warren and Lorraine Kimble's home lend themselves to mixing and matching in an ever-changing kaleidoscope of color and composition. Establishing a basic color palette comprised of traditional Colonial-era favorites, from barn red to Williamsburg blue, enables Warren to find a niche almost anywhere for the numerous treasures he brings home on a regular basis.

One of the rewards of being an expert on antiques is that Warren can spot inexpensive but valuable pieces at auctions and flea markets. The primitive cloth doll (above), was one such find. It purposely has no facial features and is likely of Amish origin, a group whose religious convictions include belief that it is irreverent to replicate faces "made in the image of God."

Warren Kimble finds great satisfaction in acquiring collectibles like the carved wood bunnies which may have only sentimental value and making them right at home with one-of-a-kind antiques.

52

With subjects ranging from animals to berries and barns to the
Stars and Stripes, it is not surprising that Warren Kimble is also an accomplished
painter of ships and seascapes. But these nautical images demonstrate
more than just painterly skill. After completing the painting "Sailor Bear"
(above), Warren realized that the sailboat images in the background of the painting
came from the wallpaper in the room he slept in as a child.

Warren still treasures his childhood companions—stuffed animals of all
shapes and sizes. As an adult, his collection has grown to include
valuable German-made bears with the original Steiff toy company tag still intact.

For centuries, the pineapple has

been a sign of hospitality.

This impressive nineteenth-century

four-poster pineapple bed

complete with canopy is a

welcome addition to the Kimble's

guest room. Other prized

antiques for guests to enjoy

include the porcelain doll, the

framed paper cutout, and a

needlework sampler. The unique

"Penny Rug Bed Covering"

handcrafted by R. C. Bowen

from heavy woolens, replicates

the penny rugs with pen wipers

that were also popular

during the nineteenth century.

Basket-making is an art, but even greater skill and creativity is required to incorporate a nature scene like the one shown here into the weaving. With dozens of rare and unusual baskets in his collection, Warren Kimble counts this one featuring rabbits at play as one of his all-time favorites.

Several years ago at an auction, Lorraine Kimble found an old hooked rug rolled up in burlap. Upon closer inspection, she discovered to her delight that the rug had been hooked in an unusual agate design with the folk artisan's name—"Loraine"—featured in the center. (A close up of just the center portion is shown here.) The entire restored rug is prominently displayed on a wall in the Kimble's home.

Warren Kimble's collection of Christmas keepsakes comes out every holiday season to be enjoyed by family and friends.

Since he creates imaginative new images nearly every day, Warren Kimble is intrigued by toys and collectibles that are just a bit out of the ordinary. He especially treasures handmade gifts from friends like the duo shown above. The stuffed roly poly bears all dressed up as a Santa and a snowman are gifts from someone who shares Warren's love of wit and whimsy.

The smiling snowman (above) is a cheerful addition to a stocking handmade by Warren's friend, Barbara Bond, to commemorate the success of his original painting of the "Snow Family" (below). This image is popular in wintertime as a widely-distributed art print and appears on numerous other licensed products including plump, oversized accent pillows.

Warren Kimble has always enjoyed

collecting the works of fellow artisans,

and with his love for circus memorabilia

as strong as ever, it became imperative for

him to acquire this antique nickelodeon

hand-painted by Marlene Coble.

A longtime admirer of circus entrepreneur

P. T. Barnum, Warren Kimble believes

these and other "collectibles of the future"

are a perfect way to celebrate the past.

In Colonial New England, religion influenced almost every aspect of daily life—especially
for the Calvinists and Quakers who rarely used anything but the Bible as their source of
guidance. Illustrated stories from the Bible proliferated, but an itinerant sign painter,
Edward Hicks, who later became a Quaker preacher in Newtown, Pennsylvania,
popularized animals through his painting of "The Peaceable Kingdom" and "Noah's Ark."
In accordance with the strict religious observance of Sunday as a day of rest, even
children were not allowed to play since it was considered a form of work. However, it
was permissible to play with biblically-inspired toys, and wooden carvings of Noah's Ark
and the animal pairs became the norm for children's Sunday afternoon playtime. Warren
Kimble's original painted mirror-image of animal pairs stands watch over his smaller set
of handcarved animals and Noah's Ark (looking much like a New England stone house).
Warren Kimble's play set is completely portable by the clever use of an antique wooden
bread bowl for the Ark's base. When not in use, the deck lifts up for storing the animals.

Inspired by his childhood love for the circus and admiration for P. T. Barnum, Warren Kimble continues to collect circus memorabilia, including the mirrored carousel panel featuring a child with sand pail playing by the seashore.

Displayed on the wall of his studio above a large collection of sand pails, the panel is a constant reminder for Warren Kimble of the happy memories he holds of summers spent building sand castles by the sea.

Which came first, the chicken painting or the chicken collectible? With Warren Kimble, it's a toss up. His folk art paintings of chickens and roosters developed at the same time as his interest in collecting these whimsical barnyard creatures from artisan friends or at auction houses. In a primitive pine cupboard in a corner of the Kimble dining room, a sample of Warren Kimble's original paintings and collection of feathered friends overflows the shelves.

Antique sand pails once used

for building sand castles

can be merely stored on

shelves to gather dust, or—

with a little imagination—

filled with sand again and used

with votives to brighten

up the garden on a

warm summer evening!

In the American colonies, houses were small and sparse and space was considered a luxury. (Citizens were taxed for having closets in their rooms!) The solution? Large wooden cupboards and massive wardrobes were handcrafted and used for storing everything from kitchenware to clothes which otherwise hung from pegs on the wall. When Warren Kimble began collecting, he chose to preserve these valuable pieces of American history, but brightened them considerably with the addition of his paintings of landscapes with houses and barns.

The strong presence of religion in early American communities resulted in churches of a variety of denominations being built in almost every town. While many of these buildings were relatively small, the pulpits of these churches were often large and ornate. Warren Kimble discovered the perfect use for these relics— plant stands with his signature trees painted on each of the inset panels.

Warren Kimble's early influences from childhood all come together in this corner "memories" grouping.

In the foreground, an unusual "Flying Geese" quilt from Warren Kimble's collection rests on an antique wooden quilt stand. On the wall, an ornate wooden frame with carved wooden leaves displays a treasured family photo of his ancestors gathered at the Kimble Family Farm.

For Warren, surrounding himself with quilts, collectibles, and keepsakes helps to keep him grounded. With his roots firmly anchored in the past, but always looking forward to the future, Warren Kimble is free to express himself creatively and, ultimately, share his gifts and talents with others.

These simple heart-of-the-home influences are amply evident in Warren Kimble's well-known painting of a "House with Quilt."

Warren Kimble's enthusiastic celebration of the spirit of America—patriotism—accompanied by his passion for collecting relics of early American history begins with hard-to-find antique advertising sculptures used as signage for Colonial shop owners. To date, Warren Kimble's collection consists of a proud Native-American Chief, a flag-waving Uncle Sam, an oratorical Abraham Lincoln with the Gettysburg Address in hand, and a properly uniformed Patriot.

The patriotic sculptures in Warren Kimble's growing collection of cigar-store figures echo historical monuments of another time and another place. In the mid-nineteenth century, when few people could read or write, shopkeepers hung out signs with unique carvings to advertise their wares. These shop signs were designed to catch the eye and make an immediate association with the product, similar to trademarks and brand names used in today's advertising.

With the decline of ship building, unemployed figurehead carvers turned to carving shop signs. The proprietors of cigar stores began hiring these carvers to make life-size wooden sculptures of Native Americans which would become widely recognized as "cigar-store Indians." For novelty's sake, they started carving sculptures of various personalities such as Uncle Sam and Abraham Lincoln as well as soldiers, sailors, and characters from literature, history, and popular culture. Often the sculpture was mounted on a base with wheels so it could be rolled inside for protection from theft and the elements. Increased literacy eliminated the need for these advertising sculptures and by the 1880s they had faded into history. The few sculptures that survive today are still afforded that same protection from theft and the elements in museums and private collections such as Warren Kimble's shown in full on the previous pages.

In the early Colonial home, rugs were everywhere but on the floor! Instead clean
sand, sifted and swept fresh daily into graceful patterns, covered the floors. "Ruggs"
(as they were called), covered beds, tables, trunks and dresser tops. Made from old
woolen clothing or blankets, penny rugs were named after large copper pennies
used as patterns for cutting hundreds of circles from tightly woven wool. Since
nothing was wasted in Colonial days, even the tiniest scraps could be salvaged by
using half-inch diameter pennies as a pattern for the smaller circle to be sewn to
the center of each large circle using the feather or buttonhole stitch. For a final
touch of practicality, individual woolen "tongues" were added as a border for use as
pen wipers, since each could be easily replaced after serving its usefulness.

Once as popular as hand-hooked rugs—especially in New England and the
state of Pennsylvania—the mix of colors and charming designs of
woolen penny rugs, like the one above (designed by Barbara Bond)
were a cheerful substitution for fresh flowers during the long harsh winters.

FOLK CRAFTS
INSPIRATIONS
With Patterns

For Warren Kimble, appreciating and acquiring interesting antiques and collectibles is only half the fun. His pleasure comes from creating his own folk crafts and inspirations for the enjoyment of others. Drawing from many of the nineteenth-century Colonial influences, Warren mixes and matches styles, colors, and textures for unique one-of-a-kind designs such as the practical "picnic" storage chest (opposite). Modeled after the Shaker nesting boxes of yesteryear, the view looking down from the top of the pyramid of drawers is a composite of strawberries and watermelon on a checkerboard tabletop complete with a fitting tribute to Warren Kimble's wry sense of humor. The bottom drawer features the ever-present picnic ants.

In Colonial America, patchwork

was a means of mending or

using scraps of fabric for

long-lasting household utility

quilts. But the challenge was

to create a useful quilt with a

collage of color that was also

pleasing to the eye. For folk artist

Warren Kimble, today's creative

challenge is to adapt an

authentic patchwork effect to a

painted surface. His successful

artistic achievement is evident

in this impressive cupboard.

Warren Kimble never tires of finding just the right piece of collectible folk art like the small lidded chest (above) and embellishing it with just the right painted motif. The completed painting should look as if it is original to the antique piece.

The first step in the process is to tape off the border using strips of masking tape. Then Warren Kimble adds a base coat of white or black gesso depending on the desired results. The undercoating of gesso provides a surface to which the acrylic Winsor & Newton paints adhere while still allowing the rough, distressed texture of the original wood to show.

Once the gesso has dried, Warren Kimble selects a motif—in this case a simple landscape—and first paints the background. When that is dry, he adds his signature trees and a rustic fence to the rolling hills of the surrounding countryside.

While he may paint variations on this seemingly simple pastoral scene time and time again, it is his artist's eye and unique style which creates the appeal and longing for the more tranquil past of yesteryear.

· ·

Like most artists, Warren Kimble spends a considerable amount of time mixing the perfect palette of paint colors to achieve the timeworn effect for his paintings. A sampling of his favorite folk colors includes shades of blue, green, yellow, gold, red, rust, white, brown, purple and black.

Reminiscent of yesteryear's decorative penny "rugg" complete with a pen-wiper border, this modern-day translation features an adaptation of Warren Kimble's original painting of nesting hens. Sized for a tabletop, the texture and dimension of the penny rug is a welcome addition to the breakfast room, complementing the companion nesting hens border of Warren Kimble's collection for Imperial Wallcovering. (To make your own Nesting Hen Penny Rug, turn to page 110 for patterns and instructions.)

Folk art images inspired by Warren Kimble's original paintings provide endless possibilites for country-style decorating. Here the animals are out of the barn and onto V.I.P. Fabric panels from Cranston. Warren's charming landscape scenes are pre-printed on fabric for quick pillows, border trims, and covered-buttons for tab curtains. Enlarge and adapt one of the animals like the cat shown here, to make a shaped pillow of your own design.

"Off the wall" art prints are fun decorating accents when you take a little time to think outside the box. Instead of the usual framed wall decor, create your own customized chalk board featuring an inexpensive art print, such as Warren Kimble's smiling "White Persian Cat."

Start with a purchased chalkboard or cut a rectangle of Masonite (ours is 10" x 24"). Sand edges smooth and add a coat of chalkboard paint or a thin layer of cork to make a memo board.

Finish with a border of gold paint or fabric trim and interesting old buttons you'd like to display. Braid a length of fabric to glue to the top for hanging and cover it with a row of buttons from your collection.

Since Warren Kimble's folk art themes range from animals to landscapes, you can choose the theme that best suits your decorating style.

Let your decorating theme spark your imagination, and like Warren Kimble you can begin a collection that will last a lifetime!

When you do choose a decorating theme, the more the merrier. Here it is cats, cats, and more cats! The Jellicoe Cats by Kathy Schammel (shown opposite) are joined by two of Warren Kimble's first fabric cats. This diverse grouping of collectibles (shown above) and reproductions created from Warren Kimble's original paintings is a classic example of how effective a single theme can be in combination with unifying colors, texture, and shape. Notice how the cat image first seen smiling on a chalkboard repeats the same welcoming smile on the fringed woven throw featured here, and the black-and-white cat pillow in the yellow rocking chair on the previous page is replicated in the rug on the floor featuring "Fat Cat."

Adapted from Warren Kimble's original painting on wood, this fabric wallhanging takes on a contemporary flair. (Turn to page 116 for patterns and instructions.) In keeping with the early folk artist's desire for balance and harmony, the artfully arranged fabric fruit basket is centered around the pineapple as a symbol of hospitality. For balance, the checkerboard basket is accompanied by not one, but two blue birds— for a double blessing of happiness!

Warren Kimble's original paintings of still life fruits and flowers, (above), demonstrate America's enduring quest for the gentle quietness portrayed in many of the primitive folk art images.

Dating back to an earlier era which offered little or no leisure time, women were able to express themselves artistically through socially approved means such as painting or needlework. They often chose familiar themes of fruit and flowers as subject matter since women were usually responsible for tending the garden which provided the food supply for the family.

In many cases, a woman's need for creative expression was greater than her artistic ability, so easily-copied patterns (templates for quilts and stencils for painting)

proliferated. In entire communities, the finished quilts and paintings often reflected the most popular pattern being copied.

The fruits of Lorraine Kimble's labors are amply evident in the gardens which thrive under her watchful care and seemingly boundless energy. Shown in the background, Warren's supply of painted fruits and florals seems boundless, too, with spectacular wooden pieces large enough to fill an exterior wall of the house.

· ·

With a little imagination, inexpensive art prints can be framed with
almost anything—even a background of galvanized steel! Here,
Wild Apple Graphics prints of Warren Kimble's original still life paintings are
framed against a background of galvanized steel on standard-issue water
containers for the garden—a tall flower bucket and watering can made
new to look old. The secret is to cover the galvanized steel with a coating of
black gesso topped by acrylic paints in artist's colors of Burnt Sienna and
Yellow Ochre for the bucket and Payne's Grey and Metallic Gold for the
watering can. After you've painted or sponged the water container, allow it to
dry thoroughly. Choose an art print small enough to appear "framed" on the side
of the bucket or watering can. Center it on one side of the bucket or of the
watering can, and glue securely. Add a sponging of paint to the edges of the
art print. Cover the surface of the art print and the galvanized steel with
several coats of clear acrylic varnish for an antique, decoupaged effect.

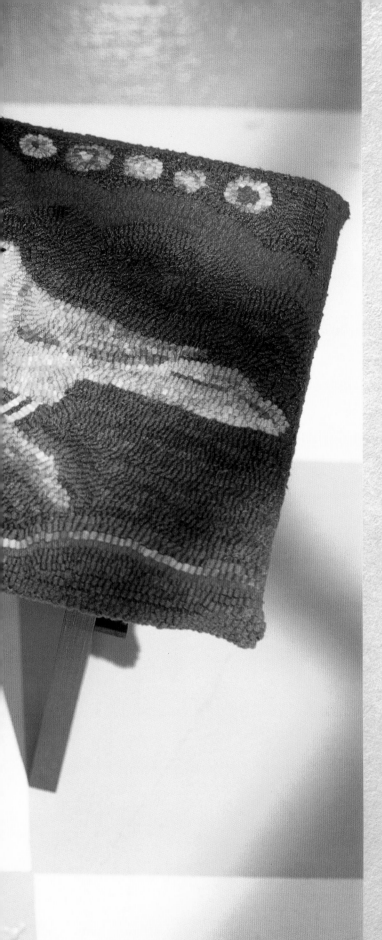

When Warren Kimble started

painting the floor of the

front hall of his home, little did he

realize that the resulting folk art

fantasy of birds and the tree of

life would inspire the design

of this hand-hooked rug.

Turn to page 122 for

patterns and instructions for

hooking your own handmade

and handsome rug,

bench- or foot-stool cover.

As the rural landscape began to fill with landmarks such as barns and one-room schools, primitive folk artists who often had more imagination than talent painted stylized renditions. These captured the essence, but not necessarily the exactness of the pastoral setting. The multi-story "Townhouse" painted by contemporary folk artist, Marlene Coble, mirrors that artistic abandon. Many of these early scenes were painted on large boards and displayed over the mantel or doorway of a drab Colonial home for decoration like Warren Kimble's original painting shown here.

One of the secrets of successful decorating is to start with several small items for big group impact. Here, a tabletop arrangement of Warren Kimble's framed original landscapes are right at home with even smaller framed originals of his favorite animal subjects bounding up the stairs.

One of his favorite frames, painted in forest green with black corner blocks (shown above), is modeled after the same technique in which many patchwork quilts are assembled— with the completed pieced block set into a fabric "frame" of corner blocks and sashing strips. Another is painted "barn" red to accentuate the unusual multi-story barn it frames.

Create your own "small but mighty" tabletop grouping with a miniature chair and lidded chest by starting with unfinished wooden pieces from Walnut Hollow. For the chair, begin by covering it with a base coat of Ultramarine Blue artist's paint and allow to dry thoroughly. Then brush on a crackle medium according to the manufacturer's directions. Allow to dry, and finish with a top coat of Aqua artist's paint.

For the lidded chest, begin by covering the box (including the ball feet) and the lid with a base coat of black gesso and allow to dry thoroughly. Paint all surfaces with Burnt Carmine artist's paint and allow to dry. Cut a section of wallpaper border with a pattern repeat from Warren Kimble's collection for Imperial Wallcoverings and use white craft glue to secure it to the outside of the box. Sponge with Cobalt Blue artist's paint, blending the top and bottom edges of the wallpaper strip.

Top off the lid with a small print such as Warren Kimble's "School House" or a section of wallpaper. Cover with clear acrylic varnish.

Transform a plain pine doll wardrobe into a conversation piece. Paint, wallpaper, and fabric scraps are all you need to make a charming miniature countertop cupboard for the kitchen or dining room side table.

Start with a piece of doll furniture like the wardrobe from Walnut Hollow (shown opposite). Cover it with a base coat of black gesso and allow to dry thoroughly. Then sponge or paint in folk art colors to match your decor. For the wardrobe door fronts, cut a scrap of wallpaper border to fit each door. For easier application, first remove the knobs and replace them later. (We used a section of a landscape border from Warren Kimble's "Barns" collection for Imperial Wallcoverings that lends itself to a seam in the center for the door openings.)

Cover the wallpaper with several coats of clear acrylic for an antique decoupage effect.

Use wallpaper or a piece of fabric to line the inside of the wardrobe. (We used a landscape scene from Warren Kimble's collection for Cranston's V.I.P. Fabrics.)

Complement the completed miniature countertop cupboard with collectibles featuring similar themes. Here, accessory pieces from the "Barns" collection for Sakura include the cookie jar, cream pitcher, sugar bowl, and salt and pepper shakers tucked inside.

A long-standing fascination for marionettes prompted Warren Kimble to collect them as well as create his own folk-art versions from scraps of pine. But for the visiting grandchildren, what good is a marionette without a stage? It didn't take long to dream up "Pop Pop's Theatre"—a fast and fun portable stage that fits easily in the doorway of the family room.

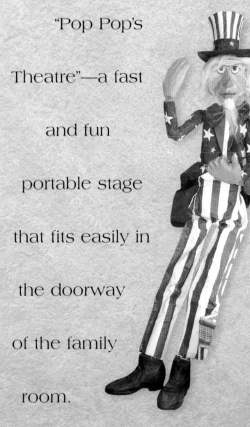

When the grandchildren visit, "Pop-Pop's Theatre" offers twice the fun when a quick turn of the sign transforms it into a store for small shoppers looking for big bargains (and candy!) from their favorite shopkeeper Warren Kimble.

On the Fourth of July, the fun moves outdoors to the expansive deck of Warren Kimble's barn studio. Gathered with son Chris and his wife Donna, and daughter Elizabeth and her husband Peter, Warren and Lorraine Kimble enjoy their grandchildren, Heather, Kevin, Hannah and Jacob, who join them in extending a spirited red, white and blue welcome to their patriotic-themed celebration.

For Warren and Lorraine Kimble, the Fourth of July is almost an everyday event celebrated in true red, white and blue style. Here, they share the view with Samantha, their West Highland Terrier nicknamed appropriately enough "Sam." Furnishings in their home and barn studio reflect Warren Kimble's keen interest in patriotism.

Highly sought after collectibles, such as the almost life size sculpture of Uncle Sam by New England artist Christopher Lamontagne (shown in the background above), inspire many of Warren Kimble's paintings.

Sometimes Warren Kimble's

inspirations for folk crafts are so

surprisingly simple that

you'll find yourself asking,

"Why didn't I think of that?"

For example, blending the old

with the new, Warren Kimble's

swirl of antique bunting used

for political rallies around the

turn of the century is right at

home draped on a picnic table.

Freshly painted with stars and

stripes and distressed to

look old, the table is home to his

brand-new collection of

patriotic "Colonial" pattern

dinnerware for Sakura.

For a touch of nostalgia, park your picnic gear in an old red wagon. Bring along a practical centerpiece for the table—a heavy-duty tote bag with a patriotic theme like this one featuring a flag adapted from Warren Kimble's original painting. Fill it with miniature flags and a Mason jar of fresh-picked flowers. Wrap the silverware in checkered napkins and tuck into the tote bag pocket for a handy buffet.

When asked by the manufacturer to choose a theme that would have instant recognition and appeal, Warren immediately decided to create a flag-inspired design for the pocket of the canvas tote by Toland Enterprises. This challenge required making the motif as simple as possible, but still readily recognizable. The result—stars and stripes that speak for themselves.

With new crafting options like rubber stamps and acrylic fabric paints, you can personalize almost anything, including Warren Kimble's canvas tote. Create your own patriotic constellation by stamping stars randomly as desired.

red, white & blue

Yes, you can take it with you! Frame your favorite memories in a rustic
barn board look-alike from Walnut Hollow. After applying a base coat of
white gesso, paint the unfinished wood in colors of your choice.
The oversized frame offers a wide expanse for adding custom trims and accents.

For the finished folk art frame shown above, the small red hearts surrounding
a keepsake photograph of Warren and Lorraine Kimble are a simple
expression of their shared sentiment that "two hearts are better than one."

The old adage, "Necessity is the mother of invention," certainly applies to the origin of these whimsical folk-art hearts created by Warren Kimble for his wife, Lorraine. As Warren recalls, he was so wrapped up in his work that to his dismay it was Valentine's Day and evening was fast approaching. Rather than rushing out to buy a last-minute card, he decided it would be easier to run down the basement, quickly cut out a heart shape from wood, and inscribe it with his own love note. Sure enough, it was a big hit with Lorraine. So much so, that with each passing year, Warren Kimble must remember to get an even earlier start on Valentine's Day—by dreaming up a new folk-art heart for Lorraine's ever-growing collection!

PATTERNS

Nesting Hen Penny Rug

Dimensions: 15" x 17"
(excluding pen-wiper tongues)

Materials

Assorted wool scraps:

15" x 17" cream for background

■

4" x 15" blue-green for scallops

■

3" x 15" teal for scallops

■

18" x 18" square of dark brown for borders

■

5" x 9" rust for chicken's body

■

9" x 9" charcoal for head, neck and feathers

■

8" x 8" pink for feathers

■

2 1/2" x 10" salmon for lower border

■

2 1/2" x 10" tan for lower border

■

3" x 3" red for comb, eye and wattle

■

3/8"-diameter
white circle for eye center

■

30 4" x 4" squares of assorted
solids & plains for pen-wiper tongues

■

15" x 17" rectangle of felt for backing

■

Embroidery floss or perle cotton:
brown, black, gray, red, yellow, pink,
coral, tan, blue, and blue-green

Directions

1. Cut out appliqué pieces for the chicken using the templates on the following pages. Refer to the Color Key for fabric choices.

2. Quilt the cream background with running stitches using the chicken wire quilting pattern. Place rust chicken body in center of cream background, 4" from the lower edge and 3 1/2" from the right edge. With brown embroidery floss or perle cotton, secure the chicken body to the background with blanket stitches.

3. With blanket stitches, add tail and wing feathers, head/neck, comb, eye and wattle. Add feather stitches or running stitches to the centers of the feathers, and five straight stitches in the comb. Refer to the Color Key for colors of wool and stitches.

4. Add white eye center, using a blind stitch and white thread. With black thread, add a French Knot for the eye's pupil. Satin stitch the beak with yellow. Using long straight stitches, stitch the "straw" to the left and right of the chicken, referring to the Color Key.

5. To create the lower border, cut each of the salmon and tan strips into 4 equal pieces, each 2 1/2" x 2 1/2". Arrange the salmon squares across the background just below the chicken and starting 1" from the right edge. Overlap the salmon squares with the tan squares; place the tan square on the left 1" from the left edge. Stitch across the top of the salmon squares with tan blanket stitches and around the top and sides of the tan squares with brown stitches.

6. From the blue-green wool, cut a 4" x 15" strip for the upper border; cut slightly irregular scallops along one edge. Blanket stitch scalloped edge to the cream background with blue-green stitches. From the teal wool, cut a 3" x 15" strip; cut slightly irregular scallops along one edge. Place on top of blue-green strip, blanket stitch lower edge with teal stitches.

7. From the brown wool, cut two side strips, each one 14" x 12 1/4"; one top strip, 3/8" x 16 1/2", and one lower strip, 2" x 16 1/2". Stitch each of the four border strips in place, then stitch the inner edges of the strips with brown blanket stitches and the outer edges with black blanket stitches.

8. Using the template on the following pages, cut 30 pen-wiper tongues (includes 1/2" allowance along straight edge to attach tongues to background). Refer to Color Key for fabric choices. Stitch around the curved edges of the pen-wiper tongues with blanket stitches in coordinating colors of floss. Arrange tongues as desired around the outside and baste in place. For finishing, hand stitch backing to wrong side of completed penny rug.

Color Key

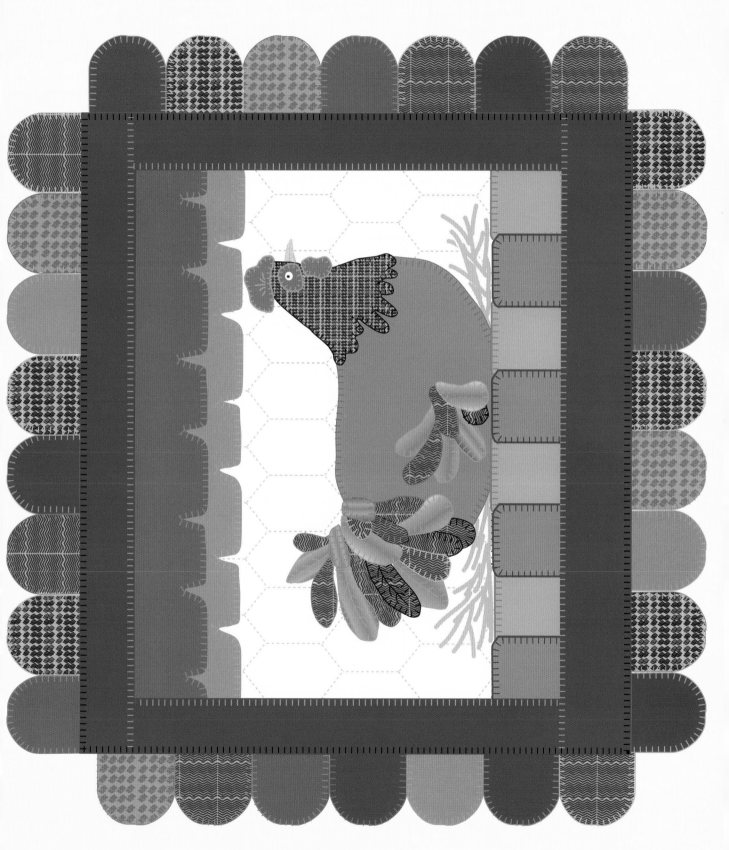

Patterns

Chicken Body

Chicken
Wire
Quilting
Pattern

Chicken
Head/Neck

Patterns

Comb

Wing
Feathers

Eye

Beak

Wattle

Pen-Wiper
Tongue

Patterns

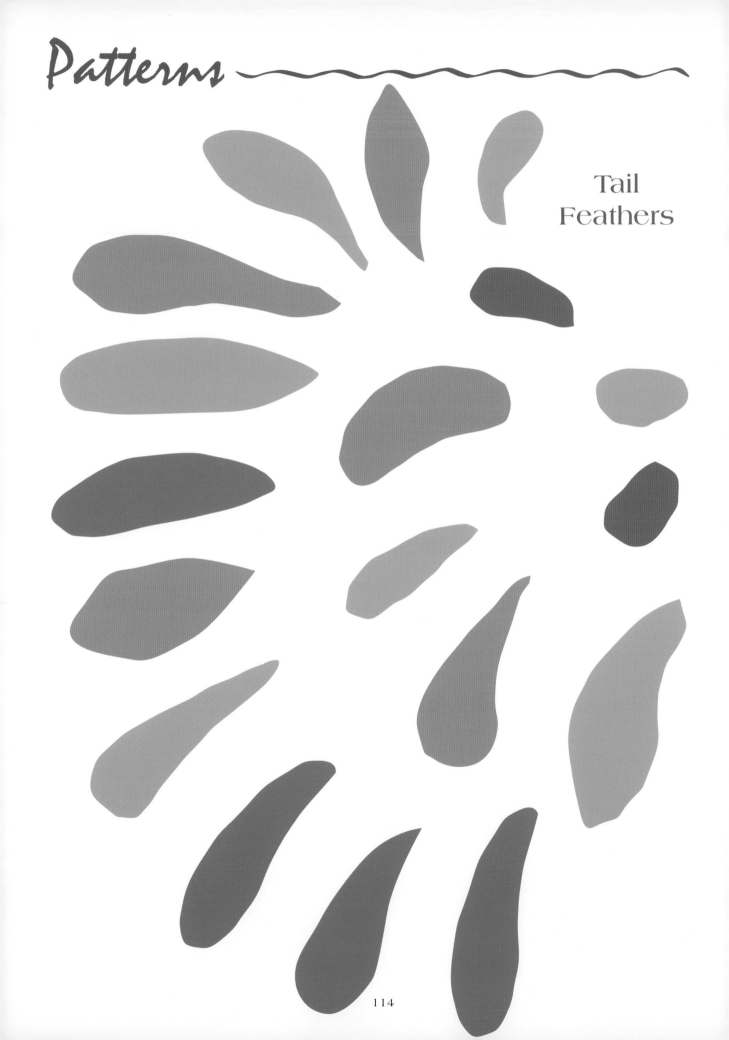

Stitching

Buttonhole Stitch / Blanket Stitch

1. To make the stitch, bring your needle and perle cotton up through the fabric at A. With your left thumb hold the perle cotton flat against the fabric at point A and to the left. Go down at B and up at C.
2. With the next stitch, point C becomes point A and you repeat the original stitch.

Running Stitch

1. Bring the needle up at A. Insert the needle in and out of the fabric as in general sewing, taking several stitches at the same time.

Feather Stitch

Imagine a straight line on the fabric where you are stitching. This imaginary line serves as a guide as you sew individual stitches on either side of the line.

1. Starting at the top of the imaginary line, bring the needle up through the fabric at A and down at B, holding the perle cotton loose on top of the fabric with your left thumb to form a loop from A to B. Allow the perle cotton to curve gently, but not twist.
2. Come up at C, keeping the perle cotton under the needle. This is the point of the "V" formed by the perle cotton from A to B.

Imaginary line

French Knot Stitch

1. Bring the needle and perle cotton up at A. Pull the perle cotton taut with your left hand. Wrap the perle cotton around the needle once, keeping it flat. More wraps will make a larger knot.
2. Insert the needle at B and pull the perle cotton so the knot is pushed close to the fabric. Keep the tension even, but do not pull too tightly or you will be unable to pull the needle through the knot and the fabric. If you leave the perle cotton too loose an unwanted loop will appear at the knot.
3. Pull the perle cotton down at B. Keep holding the perle cotton taut until most of the perle cotton has been pulled through.

Stem Stitch

This stitch is ideal for outlining large areas.

1. Begin the stitch by bringing your needle up at A. Hold the perle cotton flat on the fabric with your thumb to either side of the stem line. Regardless of which side you choose to begin your stitching, remember to stay on the same side with the rest of your stitches.
2. Before pulling the A to B stitch flat to the fabric, bring the needle up at C. Tighten the stitch. C now becomes A for the next stitch. Continue, slightly overlapping the previous stitch until the desired length of the stem is reached.

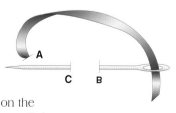

Satin Stitch

The satin stitch is a series of straight stitches done side by side to completely cover a specified area. The stitch is most beautiful when it is uniform and smooth.

1. Bring the needle up at A, then down at B. This completes one stitch. Keep the perle cotton flat, making sure that each stitch is close to, but not overlapping, the previous stitch. The distance from A to B is variable for each stitch, depending on the space or the area you need to cover.

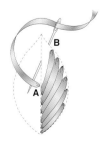

Fruit Basket Wallhanging

Dimensions: 24" x 24"

Materials

1 gold rectangle,
14 1/2" x 18 1/4", for background

◾

1 dark green rectangle,
4 1/4" x 18 1/4", for background

◾

3 red strips,
each 1 1/2" x 40"-42", for strip-pieced vase

◾

1 red strip, 1 1/2" x 20",
for strip-pieced vase lower section

◾

2 light blue #1 strips, each 1 1/2" x 40",
for strip-pieced vase upper section

◾

1 light blue #2 strip, 1 1/2" x 20",
for strip-pieced vase lower section

◾

1 dark blue strip, 1 1/2" x 40",
for strip-pieced vase center section

◾

Assorted scraps (minimum size 6" x 6")
of 3 golds, 3 dark greens,
medium blue, purple, and red

◾

4 brown strips,
each 1 1/4" x 22", for inner border

◾

4 dark red strips,
each 2 1/4" x 26", for outer border

◾

1 dark red rectangle, 26" x 26", for backing
1 rectangle, 26" x 26", of batting

◾

1/4 yard dark red
(or 100" of 2"-wide strip) for binding

◾

Assorted thread to match:
green, gold, red, purple, light blue

◾

Embroidery floss: gold, yellow,
black, brown, dark red, and purple

Directions

Note: All seam allowances are 1/4" wide, unless otherwise specified. Do not add seam allowances when cutting around pieces to be machine appliquéd.

1. Basket top section: Stitch two of the 40"-42"-long red strips, to two light blue #1 strips, alternating colors. Press seam allowances toward the first strip. Cut across this strip-pieced unit at 1 1/2" intervals.

2. Join 12 of the segments end to end to make 6 pairs, alternating colors. Stitch 3 single units and 6 pairs together to make a checkerboard unit.

3. Pin basket top section pattern on the diagonal to the checkerboard; cut around the pattern.

4. Basket body section: Stitch the remaining 40"-42"-long red strip to the dark blue strip. Press seam allowances toward the first strip. Cut across this strip-pieced unit at 1 1/2" intervals.

5. Alternating colors, join segments to make 3 rows as shown; sew rows together.

6. Pin basket body section pattern to this checkerboard unit; cut around pattern.

7. Basket base section: Stitch the 20"-long red strip to the 20"-long light blue #2 strip. Cut across this strip-pieced unit at 1 1/2" intervals.

8. Alternating colors, stitch eight segments together. Pin basket base section pattern to this unit; cut around pattern.

9. Stitch the gold and green background rectangles together along the 18 1/4" seam. Press seam allowances toward the green.

10. Cut out pattern pieces on the following pages. Trace and cut fabric appliqués, using the pattern pieces. Cut and fuse the appliqué pieces using Steam-A-Seam 2®. Arrange the basket sections, leaves, and fruit on the background. Fuse appliqué pieces following manufacturer's directions.

11. With yellow floss, embroider leaf veins, using a stem stitch. Embroider fruit details; dark red floss stem stitch for the apple; gold stem stitch for the orange and pineapple; purple for the birds' "threads." Embroider a brown French Knot at the center of each pineapple section and a black French Knot for each bird's eye.

12. Machine satin stitch around the outer edges of each appliqué piece, matching the color of thread to each appliqué piece. Use red thread around the vase sections.

13. Square up the quilt, trimming if necessary. Add brown inner-border strips, then outer dark red border strips; miter corners. Finish with 1/2" binding.

Color Key

Patterns

Basket Top

Basket Body

Basket Base

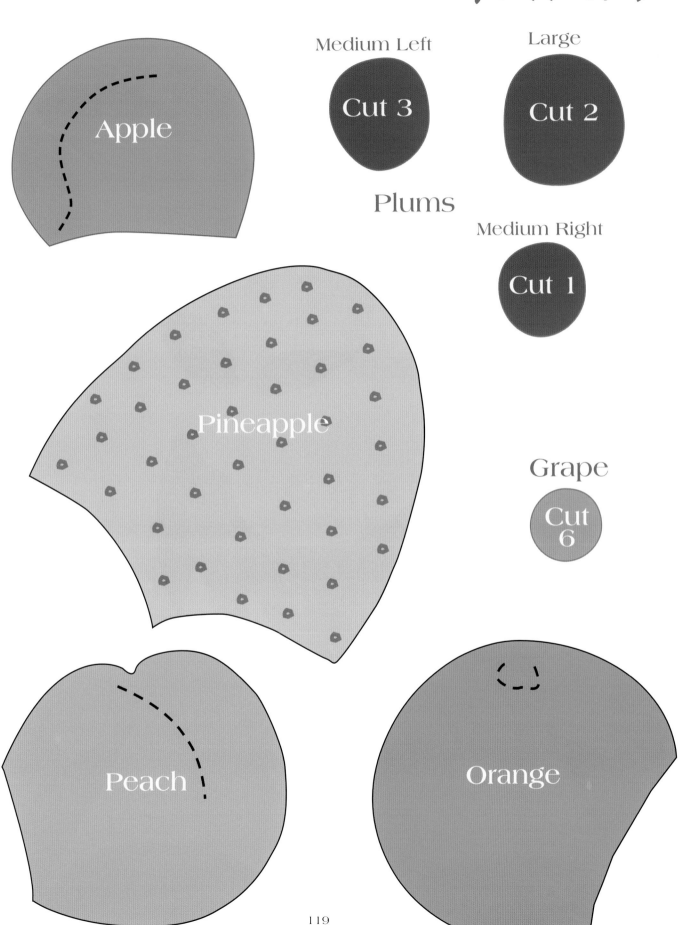

Apple

Medium Left

Cut 3

Large

Cut 2

Plums

Medium Right

Cut 1

Pineapple

Grape

Cut 6

Peach

Orange

Patterns

Leaves at
Pineapple Base

Left Plum
Leaves

Apple
Leaves

Right
Leaves

Right
Pineapple
Leaves

Left
Pineapple
Leaves

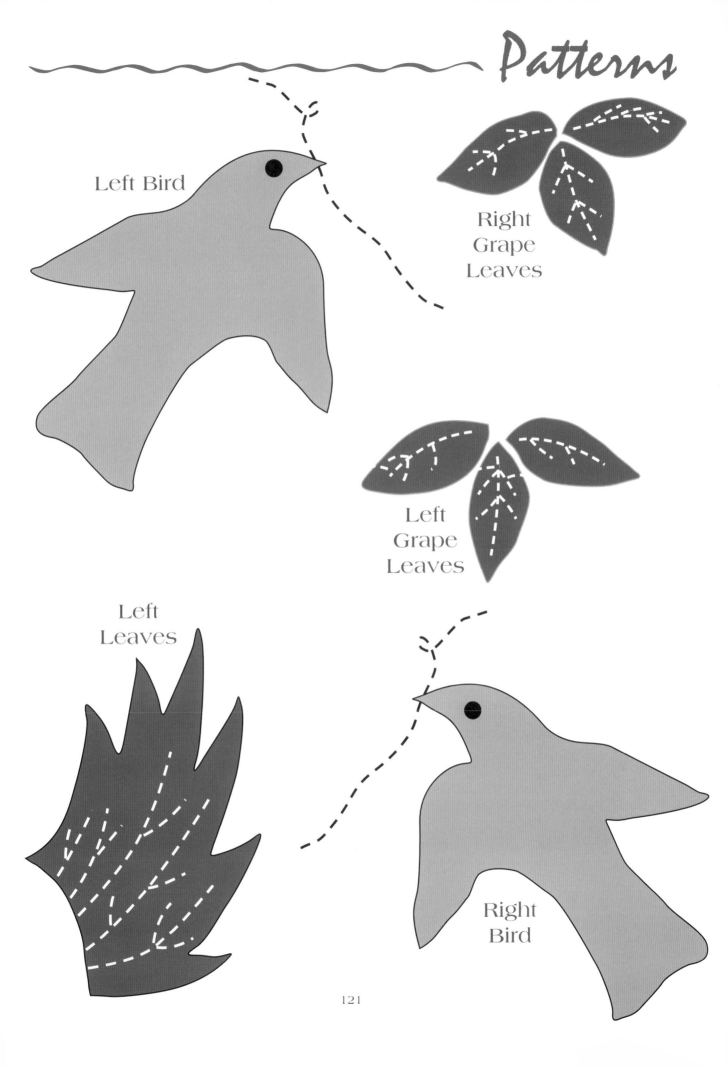

Patterns

Left Bird

Right Grape Leaves

Left Grape Leaves

Left Leaves

Right Bird

Tree of Life Hand-hooked Rug

Dimensions: 24" x 12 1/2"

Materials

Wool for hooking:
24" x 60" teal for background

■

9" x 60" rose tweed for top and bottom

■

background "frame"

■

Coral for fruit, flower centers, birds'
highlights and lower background "frame"

■

9" x 60" yellow/gold for birds and flowers

■

3" x 12" green for leaves

■

2" x 12" charcoal for trunk/stem

■

Black perle cotton for birds' eyes

■

27" x 32" rectangle of 100% cotton
Monk's cloth for rug foundation

■

Rug hook

■

Wool cutting machine

■

Embroidery hoop or
hooking frame

■

3 1/2" yds. rug tape

NOTE:
*Full-size patterns are
provided on the following pages
for making smaller hand-hooked
pieces like the 5 1/2" square
coasters shown here.*

Directions

1. Secure the edges of the Monk's cloth by turning the edge under 1/2" and stitching or zigzagging on the sewing machine.

2. Enlarge the Color Key on a copy machine to measure 24" x 12 1/2". Transfer the design to the right side of the rug using a permanent marking pen.

3. Place the rug in the embroidery hoop or hooking frame with the design side up. For best results, keep the fabric taut while you hook.

4. Cut wool for hooking using a #4 blade in your cutting machine, or cut wool by hand into 1/4"-wide strips. Begin working in a center section of the rug, referring to the step-by-step instructions for hand-hooking a rug.

5. Referring to the Color Key for placement, hook the entire rug.

Finishing

1. Staystitch or zigzag the foundation fabric 1" from the edge of the hooking; trim the excess fabric.

2. On the back of the rug, fold the corner at a 45° angle, then fold up each side to miter the corner. Slipstitch the fabric to the back of the rug.

3. If desired, sew rug tape over the foundation fabric, mitering the corners.

Color Key

1. Hold the end of a wool strip in your left hand under the fabric where you are starting. (Reverse if left-handed.) Use the hand under the fabric to guide the strip as you pull it to the top with the hook. (As you work, check with the left hand to make sure the surface is smooth and there are no loops on the back of the rug.)

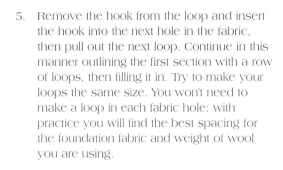

2. Insert the hook through the fabric. Catch the wool strip with the hook and bring the end of the strip up to the top of the fabric. Leave about 1/2" sticking up.

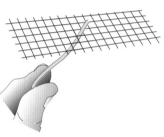

3. Insert the hook in the "hole" next to where the end of the strip is sticking up.

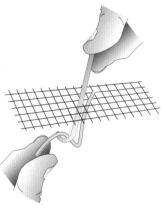

4. Grab the strip under the fabric and bring it up to the top to form a 1/4"-high loop of wool.

5. Remove the hook from the loop and insert the hook into the next hole in the fabric, then pull out the next loop. Continue in this manner outlining the first section with a row of loops, then filling it in. Try to make your loops the same size. You won't need to make a loop in each fabric hole: with practice you will find the best spacing for the foundation fabric and weight of wool you are using.

6. When you come to the end of a strip, pull the tail through to the top of the fabric.

7. Through the same hole, pull the end of the next strip, leaving about a 1/2"-long tail as you did in step 5, then continue hooking.

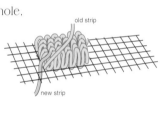

old strip

new strip

8. When you have hooked around the area where strip ends are sticking up, clip the tails even with the tops of the loops. The loops will hold the tails in place.

Sources

Warren Kimble shares his licensing success with the following group of manufacturers. For more information about specific products, contact the manufacturer listed below, or Courtney Davis, Inc., exclusive licensing agent for Warren Kimble (800/432-2614).

Calendars, stationery, magnets (Amcal: 800/824-5879); *resin giftware and kitchen accessories* (Boston Warehouse: 888/923-2982); *maple syrup and pancake mix labels* (Brown Family Farms); *handpainted and metal decorative accessories* (Cape Craftsmen: 800/436-3726); *photo frames* (Fetco International: 800/225-0465); *decorative and functional firescreens* (Fireside Designs: 828/692-1744); *paper tableware and social expressions* (C.R. Gibson: 800/251-4000); *decorative accessories, framed and signed prints* (GuildMaster: 417/869-3600); *T-shirts, tote bags, and kitchen textiles* (Heartland Trading Company: 800/299-8683); *resin decorative garden accessories* (Hen-Feathers: 800/282-1910); *"Coasterstone" coasters* (Hindostone Products, Inc.: 800/288-2191); *kitchen textiles and tabletop accessories* (Housewears, Inc.: 847-965-9400); *wallcoverings and fabrics* (Imperial Wallcoverings, Inc.: 800/222-3700); *enamel cookware, wooden pantryware, and tea kettles* (M. Kamenstein & Co.: 914/785-8023); *lifestyle books* (Landauer Publishing: 800/557-2144); *fine furnishings* (Lexington Furniture Co: 336/249-5300); *hammocks and outdoor pillows* (Magnolia Casual: 228/762-7151); *tapesty woven throws and pillows* (Manual Woodworkers & Weavers: 800/814-6597); *hooked rugs* (Nichols Hill: 404/658-0010); *jacquard woven jackets and vests* (Painted Pony: 800-894-3769); *cork-backed placemats and coasters* (Pimpernel/Impressions: 800/826-0636); *pieced comforters and pillows* (Quilt Gallery: 864/306-9888); *dinnerware and accessories* (Sakura, Inc.: 212/683-4000); *ceramic home and garden* (Santa Barbara Ceramic Design: 800/933-2529); *decorative pillows, floor mats, flags, and mousepads* (Toland: 800/989-6287); *lamps and decorative accessories* (TomLin Designs: 800/548-6425); *wooden home decor accessories* (2-Day Designs: 336/774-7085); *outdoor furniture* (Uwharrie Chair Co.: 800/934-9663); *V.I.P. Fabrics* (a division of Cranston Print Works: 800/847-4064); *open edition posters and prints* (Wild Apple Graphics: 800/756-8359); *cookbook "Country Suppers" by Ruth Cousineau, illustrated by Warren Kimble* (William Morrow Publishing: 800/237-0657).

ART GALLERY

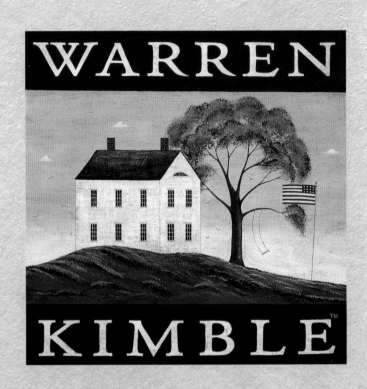